Saarah ♡.

"Thank you for making me
so wonderfully complex..."
Psalm 139:14

Saarah you are so
uniquely beautiful!
God made no one like you!
You have a wonderful mix of
gifting & personality because
He has a special and
exciting plan for your life...
Enjoy being you - simply
fully you!

Maward

Olivia & Me

Mary Ann Ward

Olivia & Me

Printed in Canada

ISBN: 978-1-4866-1462-2

Word Alive Press
131 Cordite Road, Winnipeg, MB R3W 1S1
www.wordalivepress.ca

Library and Archives Canada Cataloguing in Publication

Ward, Mary Ann, author
Olivia & me / Mary Ann Ward.

Issued in print and electronic formats.
ISBN 978-1-4866-1462-2 (hardcover).--ISBN 978-1-4866-1463-9 (ebook)

I. Title. II. Title: Olivia and me.

PS8645.A7346O45 2017 jC813'.6 C2017-902325-X
C2017-902326-8

Dedication

To dedicate a book is risky at best since there have been a multitude of unnamed encouragers whose imprint of positive support fills each page. However, I would be amiss to neglect to give immense appreciation to my husband, Keith, who always believed in me and sacrificially supported this piece. To my sons and daughters-in-love, "Thank you so much!" But the main motivators have undoubtedly been my grandchildren: Mataya, Madeline, Kasden, Miranda, Erica, Raelene, Lily, Mara, Brianna, Nolan and Alexa. Your excitement to see each page complete pressed me forward. This book would have been impossible if it had not been for the intense promptings of the Holy Spirit, pushing me beyond my own belief or comfort, and the prayers of others.

Before the earth or even time began,
We were in God's heart and in His plan.

On our very first day, who ever thought
Of the adventures unfolding from this very spot…
for Olivia and me?

We wiggled and we squiggled;
we rolled and we crawled.
We tumbled in sheer pleasure
and we laughed out loud.

Each day a discovery! Every day a delight!
But sometimes nothing seemed quite right…
to Olivia and me.

One day, unexpectedly, we spotted something new.
You saw me and I saw you.
One so little, and one so tall!
How silly you seem to me, after all…
to Olivia and me.

Sliding down hills, climbing up trees, or reaching high,
Gazing at eagles held effortless in clear blue sky…
"If only I had wings and I could soar,
Then I would see and do so much more,"
sighed Olivia and me.

One day the truth began to unfold;
The story of a cross and a tomb was told.
Such love could never–no, never–be measured,
But always, yes always, and forever treasured...
by Olivia and me.

Where could such joy ever come from
Except God the Father and Jesus, His Son?
I whirled and I spun with sheer delight
Twisting and twirling in God's great light...
Olivia and me.

The outside unchanging! Inside made new!
Invisible re-creating! God's love breaking through!
Without explanation, we knew there was more;
A greater purpose for our lives was in store…

for Olivia and me.

Of love, joy and peace
there was much to share;
With patience and kindness
life was full–without care.

Goodness and faithfulness
are not always fun,
But with gentleness and self-control
new friends are won…

*for Olivia
and me.*

A discontent called us, deep and strong,
To stretch and to reach beyond earth's ground.
"I must break free," is what we said,
as we left cocoon and unmade bed…
both Olivia and me.

Don't be fooled by what you now see!
I'm skipping down streets as free as the breeze!
Under five brilliant light-bows, chatting with friends,
with fun and with laughter, days without end…

Olivia and me.

There are mountains to climb and rivers to cross.
Of endless beauty, there is no loss.
I drink from the spring of life each day.
The Light of God keeps the night away…

for Olivia and me.

It's only just begun of adventure its clear.
I'll show you much more when you get here.
You don't need to hurry! You don't need to rush!
Eternity is forever! There is really so much…

for Olivia and me

MA Ward

"I make all things new!" He announces with force,
As He advances with His army on a great white horse.
With my armor secure and sword by my side,
My heart leaps high, His beautiful bride…

Olivia and me

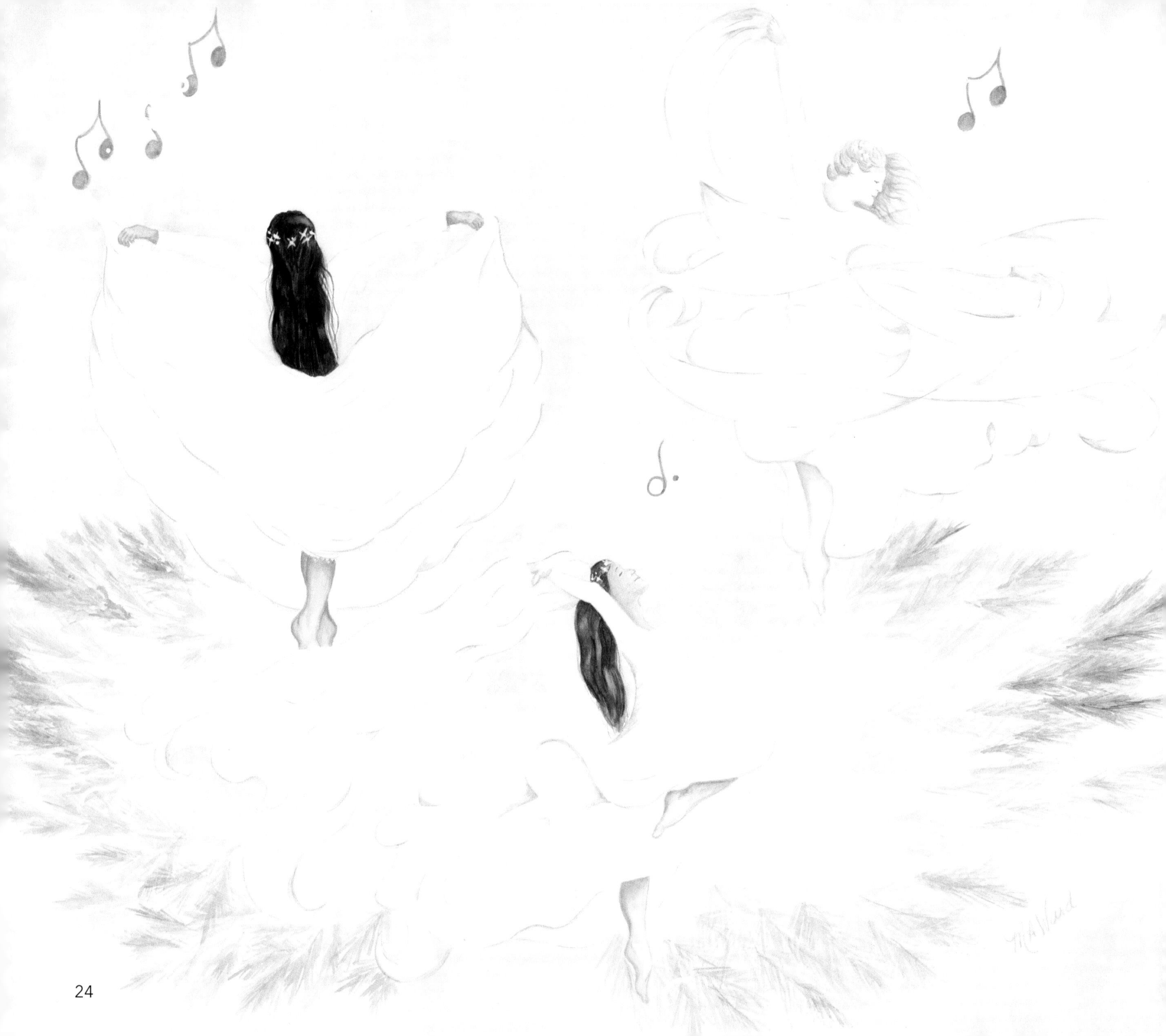

Worshipping with angels at the throne of our King–
Multitudes praise Him with the songs that they sing.
I bow in pure wonder–why, He thought of me,
And planned pure perfection for my eyes to see...

Olivia and me

Christ the Lord
Wonderful Counselor
Protector
God with us Savior
Redeemer

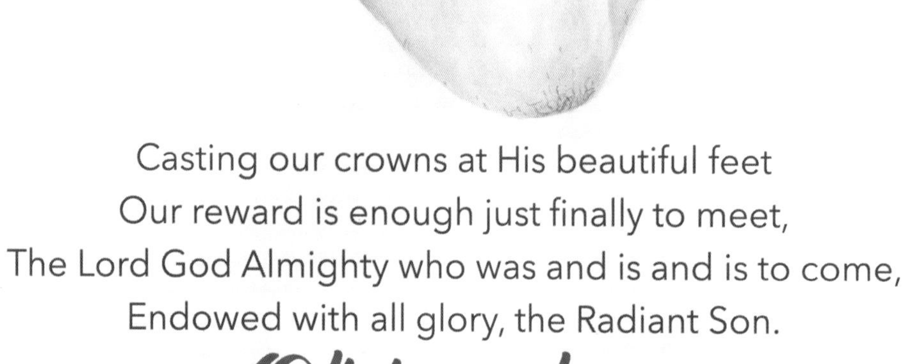

Casting our crowns at His beautiful feet
Our reward is enough just finally to meet,
The Lord God Almighty who was and is and is to come,
Endowed with all glory, the Radiant Son.

Olivia and me

Emmanuel
Holy and Exalted One
Provider
The Resurrection and The Life
Holy Spirit
Father, Son and
Potter
Prince of Peace
Messiah
Hope
The Way, The Truth and The Life
Jehovah
Good Sheperd
The Lamb
Teacher
Yahweh
My Strength and my Shield
God Most High
My Refuge
Creato
The Lord our Righteousness
Holy
The Vine
I AM
Master
Healer
Almighty
Deliverer
The Bread of Life
Ancient of D
Love
King of Glory
The Lord our Maker
The Beginning and The End
Light of The World
The Rock
Faithful and True Witness
God of all Comfort

Do you know that God saw you before you were born and that He has
a wonderful plan for your life? He loves you very much. (Psalms 139:16)
God's design and desire is for you to have an exciting and full life now and forever in heaven–
a life connected with Him. (John 10:10)
However, there is a problem! God is holy and perfect. Only those who are without sin can enjoy
His wonderful plan. The problem is that everybody sins
(that means we all do wrong things)! (Romans 3:23)
Because God loves us so much He created a solution. He sent His son, Jesus, to die on the cross to
pay the price for our sins. Jesus died on the cross for our punishment for sin. (Romans 5:8)
On the third day, Jesus rose alive from the grave! He rose to life to give us life!
Hooray! (Romans 6:23)
The Bible also says that if we believe this we can have a life in relationship with God by believing
in Jesus and what He has done for us. (Romans 10:9–10)

If you believe this and you would like to trust Jesus for forgiveness and eternal life, it is easy!
You can begin your "life to the full" today with a simple prayer:

Dear God,

I believe Jesus died on the cross for my sins. Please forgive me,
come into my life, and give me your life. I want to do my best to live for you.
In Jesus' Name,
Amen (Romans 10:13, John 20:31)

Welcome to LIFE!!! You have only begun your life in relationship with God. This relationship with
God will grow as we pray every day, talking with Him, and as we read the Bible, Him talking with us.